SOON-TO-BE
A GRANDMOTHER

From Anticipation to Embrace.
Your Guide to Navigating Grandmotherhood
with Wisdom, Grace and Love at every step.

by Nana Carolina,
Grandmother of Four

This Book Belongs To

_____

Published by Nanas Publishing House

ISBN: 978-1-927961-31-5
Library of Congress Catalog

Cover Design by Evgenyia

First Edition

10 9 8 7 6 5 4 3 2

Printed in USA

For permission requests, please contact the publisher at:

www.nanaspublishinghouse.com

The most wisdom in one place for the have it all grandmother. Stories, information, inspiration and actionable ideas from the heart to your inbox

www.moderngrandmothers.com

Dedication Page

This book is dedicated to my grandchildren ☺ my beautiful granddaughter and my three wonderful grandsons. You four are the reason I can share with other grandmothers-to-be around the world.

You are the melody in my heart and the laughter in my soul. Each of you, unique and precious, has woven your own thread into the fabric of my life, making it richer, brighter, and full of wonder.

To my granddaughter, you are a bloom in my garden, a reminder of grace and strength. Your spirit dances like a butterfly, you are a warrior, you are a healer, you are powerful, and you bring colors to my world that I never knew existed. You are my super girl, my raison d'être.

To my grandsons, each of you is a shining star, each with your own light. You are my explorers, adventurers, and dreamers, with hearts as vast as the sky and spirits as bold as the sea. Your energy and curiosity remind me daily of life's boundless possibilities.

Together, you are the heartbeat that gives my life rhythm, the joy that fills my days, and the love that overflows my heart. Thank you for teaching me the art of wonder all over again—for the love you bring, the laughter you inspire, and the legacy you are becoming.

Forever and always, with all my love,

Nanina

A Grandmothers First Embrace

"In the quiet dawn of a brand-new day,
A tiny heartbeat finds its way into the world,

The first cry, the first smile, the very first tear,
Moments like whispers that you hold dear.
A love is born beyond compare.

Eyes that sparkle, Eyes that twinkle like stars at night,
Hold the past and future in their light.
A sacred bond, a pure delight—
A love that makes the spirit take flight.

Your heart, once full, now overflows,
With joy that only a grandmother knows.

Oh, heart of mine, how can you bear
The bloom of love that blossoms there?

In that first embrace, time finds its place,
And the soul is lit by a love's embrace.

A new chapter blooms, a new story unfolds,
Little fingers curl around your own,
A bond so deep, a love well-known ignites within your very soul.

The soft weight against your chest,
The fluttering heart that knows it's blessed,
For in their breath, your soul finds rest—
A lullaby of love that sings its best.

A lifetime of wisdom, stories untold,
Now passed to the little one you hold.

A spark of the past, a glimpse of the new,
A circle complete, a journey with you.

As you welcome new life, you find your true place.
For in that small face, a world comes alive,
In the eyes of your grandchild, you truly revive.
For being a grandmother, Is a love story endless, forever, and true.

Each smile is a poem, each laugh a prayer,
Each tear a story only you share.

A first-time grandmother, where love multiplies,
In this sacred bond, where eternity lies."

-by Nana Carolina

Table of Contents

Thoughts

I still remember the day my son uttered the most joyous, terrifying, and unbelievable words that I'd ever heard: *"You're going to be a grandmother."*

I was driving down the highway when he put his hand on my shoulder and said, *"I've got something to tell you."* My heart pounded as I glanced at his wide smile, sensing that something big was coming.

"You're going to be a grandmother in December," he said.

"A wwwhhhhat?" I stammered, *"Can you repeat that?"* Laughing he repeated with even more excitement, *"You're going to have a granddaughter."*

Shock hit me, I was speechless for a moment.

I looked at his beaming smile and asked, *"Really?"* He nodded, and in that moment, I was overwhelmed with utter joy. I was going to have a granddaughter! A newborn would soon grace our home, and I'd get to witness the wonder of seeing my child become a parent.

I will never forget the euphoria that swept through my body. Once the shock wore off, over the next few hours, and even the next few days, it slowly started to sink in.

At first, I didn't feel ready to be a grandmother. I still felt young, busy with my career in the corporate world and working on my side hustles.

It just didn't seem like the right time. But that feeling quickly changed—especially when I found out it was a girl.

That day brought me the best news and the most precious gift of my life, *after my own children, that is.*

I have become the ultimate adoring grandmother. I have embraced it with every cell of my being.

I thought to myself, wow, a grandmother, but then I began to think on this, and realized something very quickly.

I am a modern grandmother; I am nothing like the grandmothers of yesteryears. And the more I investigated the grandmothers of today I realized that women of today who were also grandmothers were totally modern, they were chic, sharp, together, connected, busy entrepreneurs, CEOs, fitness gurus, you name it, grandmothers of my day were rocking it – and that is when **moderngrandmothers.com** was born.

My granddaughter turns 18 this year and before she was even born moderngrandmothers.com was born. I sat on this domain for all these years, and now guess what, she is the one inspiring me to get it out into the world. Who would have thought. *'That's your handle nana, own it"*, she said. WOW!! (#moderngrandmothers) ☺

I am so blessed, and soon you too will be blessed. Let the adventure begin ...

Who We Are – Today's Grandmothers

Powerful. Influential. Integral.

Grandmother's voices rise beyond convention.

Since becoming a grandmother (*a modern grandmother, I might add*), I have been blessed to meet an inspiring array of incredible women, who are also grandmothers *or* soon-to-be grandmothers.

Some are my neighbors, others from my community, and many I've met through my travels.

My connections with these amazing grandmothers have stretched beyond borders and oceans. Even language cannot hold back the connections I've forged with these matriarchs.

I am in awe of the countless Grandmothers I've encountered, each of them redefining what it means to be a grandmother today.

Grandmothers are a powerful force. Together, we light the way for generations to come.

We are a chorus of vibrant voices, guiding our grandchildren toward greatness.
We trust in the power of stories, woven with wisdom and love.
We are committed to the success of our grandchildren, knowing they will enrich their own lives and the lives of others.

From a single grandmother's words of encouragement, millions of grandchildren can find the strength to speak their truth.

From one cherished book, read with care by a grandmother to her grandchild, seeds of knowledge take root.
From the steady guidance of a grandmother, a child may find the courage to change their world and kindle the flames of the future.

Albert Einstein once said, *"Setting an example is not the main means of influencing others; it is the only means."* Today's Modern Grandmothers embody this truth, lifting the next generation, **one grandchild at a time.**

Here's to all the Modern Grandmothers *and* **Soon-to-be Grandmothers**—we celebrate you!

Join our tribe and embark on this incredible journey into grandmotherhood, where we empower you to not only thrive in your own life but also make a lasting, meaningful impact in your grandchildren's lives. Step into this exciting chapter with us, where you'll be supported, inspired, and equipped to be the best grandmother you can be, and continue living your best life.

www.moderngrandmothers.com

Introduction

Embrace the Joy of Becoming A Grandmother

Do you remember the first time you held your own child?

Now, imagine that multiplied by a thousand.

"**Soon-To-Be A Grandmother**" takes you on a journey to rediscover the unparalleled joys of family through the eyes of a grandmother who has been blessed to travel this road. With its heartwarming narratives and practical wisdom, this book is not just a guide but a cherished companion for those on the cusp of grandparenthood.

Ready to embark on this heartwarming journey?

Turn the pages and prepare to be enchanted by what awaits you. Your new adventure as a soon-to-be grandmother is just beginning. Don't just anticipate – **celebrate** every precious moment. Dive into this beautiful book and transform your experience into a joyous, unforgettable legacy. There is a place at the end of this book to journal your thoughts, write ideas, and jot down anything that comes to mind for your grandbaby and their parents.

Today's grandmothers are redefining what it means to be a grandmother. They are no longer just the sweet, cookie-baking figures of the past.

Instead, they are dynamic women who continue to contribute to the working world or run their own successful businesses. Balancing their professional lives with the joys of grandmotherhood, they bring the same passion and energy to both roles.

For grandmothers, embracing this new chapter in their lives it is more than just a milestone; it's a cherished opportunity to infuse wisdom, love, and a sense of adventure into their families' lives.

Many grandmothers are still actively engaged in their careers, bringing decades of experience and insight to their fields. They are CEOs, entrepreneurs, teachers, healthcare professionals, artists, and so much more. Their careers do not slow down just because they have entered a new phase of family life. Instead, becoming a grandmother fuels their drive, adding a new layer of purpose to their professional endeavors. They find themselves more motivated than ever to continue breaking barriers and setting examples not only for their children but for their grandchildren as well.

Embracing grandmotherhood brings a unique joy that is often described as unparalleled. Many grandmothers speak of the indescribable happiness they feel when they first hold their grandchild or hear that sweet little voice calling them "Grandma" for the first time.

It is a new kind of love — fierce, protective, and deeply fulfilling. Unlike the responsibilities they faced as parents, grandmotherhood allows them to focus on pure enjoyment and the creation of special bonds. They relish in the opportunity to be playful, loving, and, sometimes, a little indulgent.

In this modern era, grandmothers often have a vibrant social life and are active in their communities. They bring their grandchildren along for the ride, exposing them to a world of learning, culture, and philanthropy.

Whether they are taking their grandchildren on nature walks, teaching them about community service, or sharing their love for the arts, grandmothers are creating a legacy of values and experiences. They see themselves not only as caregivers but as guides, helping to shape the next generation in meaningful ways.

Many of these grandmothers also embrace technology, using it to stay connected with their grandchildren in ways that previous generations could not.

From video calls to social media, they bridge the gap between distance and time. They are tech-savvy and adapt to the modern tools that help them be present in their grandchildren's lives, no matter where they are. This adaptability is a testament to their willingness to learn and grow, reflecting the same curiosity and enthusiasm they hope to instill in their grandkids.

What makes today's grandmothers stand out is their ability to embrace this new phase of life with all that is in them. They understand that being a grandmother does not mean giving up on personal aspirations or ambitions. Instead, it means adding a new dimension to their identity, one that is enriched by the laughter, curiosity, and wonder of a new generation. It is a role they take on wholeheartedly, knowing that they are creating ripples that will be felt for years to come.

This new generation of modern grandmothers also takes care of themselves. They prioritize their health and well-being so that they can be active participants in their grandchildren's lives for many years. Whether it's through fitness routines, mindfulness practices, or pursuing hobbies that keep them mentally sharp, they understand that a healthy grandmother is a happy grandmother. Their focus on self-care is a powerful message to their families about the importance of living a balanced, fulfilling life.

Ultimately, today's modern grandmothers are a blend of tradition and modernity. They are torchbearers of wisdom and love, but also symbols of empowerment and resilience.

Their journey as grandmothers is filled with endless joy, new adventures, and deep, unconditional love. They embrace this role with open hearts and open minds, knowing that being a grandmother is indeed one of the most beautiful and enriching experiences life has to offer.

"Grandchildren are the
Rainbow of life.
Great-grandchildren are the
pot of gold."

Chapter One

The Announcement.

The Euphoria of Hearing the News

The moment you hear the news, it feels like the world has burst into a million tiny stars, each one shimmering with possibility and joy.

There's an immediate rush—a wave of euphoria that courses through your entire body, leaving you breathless and exhilarated. You can hardly believe it; your child is going to have a child! Your heart races with excitement, your eyes brim with tears, and your mind spins with a thousand beautiful thoughts all at once. It's a feeling unlike any other—an indescribable blend of wonder, joy, and love that fills every corner of your being.

The joy is so immense, so overwhelming, that you can hardly contain it. You want to shout it from the rooftops, share it with the world, tell every friend, neighbor, and passerby that a new life is coming into your family.

There's a sense of pride that accompanies the news—pride in your child, in your family, and in the miracle of life itself. You begin to call those closest to you, your voice trembling with happiness as you share, "I'm going to be a grandmother!" With each retelling, the joy magnifies, rippling outward like waves on a still pond. You hear the excitement in their voices, feel the love in their words, and know that this news is already bringing so much light and happiness to everyone who hears it.

In the days that follow, you find yourself floating on a cloud of happiness, as if a permanent smile has been etched on your face. Everywhere you go, you carry this secret joy, this magical anticipation that only a soon-to-be grandmother can understand.

It's the kind of joy that transforms even the most mundane moments into something extraordinary. The grocery store, the drive to work, a walk in the park—all become backdrops to your daydreams about what is to come. You picture tiny hands reaching for yours, a baby's laughter echoing through your home, and the warmth of a new generation beginning to unfold right before your eyes.

The emotions are not just in your mind—they pulse through your entire body, like a gentle current of pure happiness. You feel lighter, more alive, and deeply connected to something greater than yourself. Your heart swells with love, not just for the grandchild you have yet to meet but also for your child, who is embarking on their own incredible journey. There's a deep sense of gratitude that wells up within you—a thankfulness for this precious gift, for the chance to witness and be a part of this new life. You realize that you are about to experience one of life's greatest joys, and it fills you with a sense of awe and wonder.

And then there's the unimaginable joy—the kind that fills you up and overflows into every part of your life. It's the joy of knowing that your family is growing, that there will be new traditions to start, new memories to make, and new love to share. It's the joy that keeps you awake at night, dreaming of the future and all the beautiful moments that are yet to come. It's a joy that wraps around you like a warm embrace, reminding you that life is full of surprises, full of magic, and full of love that expands beyond measure. This joy is more than just a feeling—it's a state of being, a celebration of life that touches your soul and leaves you forever changed.

Preparing Yourself Mentally and Emotionally

Preparing yourself mentally and emotionally for becoming a grandmother is a journey of its own—a path that requires both reflection and openness. As the news sinks in, you may find yourself navigating a wide range of emotions, from pure joy and excitement to a bit of apprehension about this new role. It's essential to give yourself the space to process these feelings, to recognize that while this is a time of immense happiness, it also marks a significant transition in your life. You are stepping into a new chapter, and just like any new beginning, it comes with its own set of challenges, questions, and reflections. Embrace this time to connect with yourself, to understand what kind of grandmother you hope to be, and to prepare for the profound emotional growth that is about to unfold.

Mentally preparing yourself involves acknowledging the shift in dynamics that this new addition will bring. Your relationship with your child will evolve as they step into parenthood, and your role will also expand beyond what you've known. It's a time to reflect on your past experiences as a parent—what you cherished, what you might have done differently, and how those lessons can guide you in your new role as a grandmother.

This is also a time to build emotional resilience, understanding that there will be moments of joy, but also moments that require patience, understanding, and adaptability. By being mentally prepared, you set the stage for a supportive, loving relationship with both your grandchild, and the child's own family, who will look to you for wisdom and reassurance – sometimes.

Emotionally, becoming a grandmother is about opening your heart to a love that is both familiar and entirely new. It's about preparing to love deeply, to give freely, and to embrace the uncertainties that come with welcoming a new life into the family. It's also about being present— truly savoring each moment, from the first time you feel that baby kick through your child's belly (or your daughter in law's belly) to the moment you hold them in your arms. You'll need to prepare yourself for the waves of emotion that will undoubtedly come, from the overwhelming joy to the tender moments of watching your child become a parent. Allow yourself to feel every emotion fully, for it is through this openness that the bond between you and your grandchild will be rooted and grow, flourishing in love, connection, and understanding.

"The most precious jewels you'll ever have around your neck are the arms of your grandchildren."

Chapter Two
First Glimpse.

The Magical Moments of Meeting Your Grandchild

The first time you lay eyes on your grandchild is a moment unlike any other—a moment where time seems to slow, and the world narrows to the tiny, perfect being before you. As you enter the room, your heart races with anticipation. You've imagined this moment so many times, but nothing could prepare you for the overwhelming flood of emotion that comes rushing in. There they are, so small, so pure, a new life that carries within them the promise of the future and the legacy of the past. You feel a magnetic pull toward them, an inexplicable connection that transcends anything you've ever felt before. It's as if your heart has found a new rhythm, beating in sync with theirs.

When you first hold your grandchild in your arms, it's as though the world stops spinning for just a moment. You feel the warmth of their tiny body against yours, the gentle rise and fall of their breath, and suddenly, everything feels right. The softness of their skin, the delicate weight of their little form resting in your arms—it's a sensory symphony that plays directly to your heartstrings. Tears well up in your eyes, blurring your vision, but you don't mind. These are tears of pure, unadulterated joy, an emotional release of all the love you've been holding onto for so long. It's a love that fills every part of you, spilling over and warming the very core of your being.

As you gaze down at this new life, you see a world of possibility in their peaceful, sleeping face. You notice the tiny curve of their nose, the flutter of their eyelids, and the way their fingers curl around yours with surprising strength. In that instant, you are filled with an indescribable sense of wonder and awe. This child is a part of you, a continuation of your family's story, and yet entirely their own person. The realization hits you like a wave: this is the beginning of a new chapter, one filled with potential, discovery, and a love that knows no bounds.

A rush of memories floods back to you—memories of holding your own child for the first time, of the sleepless nights and the endless joy of watching them grow. But this is different. As a grandmother, the love you feel is pure and uncomplicated, free from the anxieties and responsibilities of parenthood. You are here to cherish, to support, and to shower this little one with all the love you have accumulated over the years. It is a liberating kind of love, one that allows you to be fully present in this magical moment, drinking in every detail, every sensation.

You feel a deep sense of gratitude wash over you—gratitude for this precious gift, for the chance to hold a new generation in your arms, and for the incredible journey that lies ahead. You are overwhelmed by the realization that you are a part of something so much bigger than yourself, a link in the chain of life that stretches back through time and will continue forward into the unknown. It's a humbling, beautiful realization that fills your heart with both pride and humility.

As you rock your grandchild gently, a sense of peace settles over you. The world outside may be full of chaos and uncertainty, but here, in this moment, there is only love. You whisper softly to them, words of welcome, of love, of promise. You promise to always be there for them, to be their safe haven, their storyteller, their biggest cheerleader. You know that from this moment on, your life will be forever changed, your heart forever expanded to make room for this incredible new love.

The tears continue to fall, but they are not tears of sadness—they are tears of overwhelming joy, of profound connection, of a love so deep it defies description. You feel a warmth spread through your chest, a mixture of pride, tenderness, and an almost sacred feeling of awe. You marvel at how someone so small could evoke such monumental emotions, how a single moment could redefine your understanding of love.

With each breath, with each tiny sigh your grandchild makes, you fall deeper in love. You are entranced by their every movement, their every sound. It's as if you are discovering a new language—one spoken in heartbeats, in soft murmurs, in the way they nuzzle closer to you, seeking comfort in your warmth. You realize that this is the beginning of a lifelong bond, a connection that will only grow deeper with time.

As you hold them, you think about all the moments to come—the first smile, the first steps, the first words. You imagine the stories you'll tell, the lessons you'll share, the adventures you'll have together. And in that imagining, you feel a profound sense of purpose, a renewed sense of vitality and excitement for the future. This little one has given you a new lease on life, a new role to embrace, and you know you will cherish every second of it.

And so, in this first embrace, you hold not just a child, but a universe of love, of potential, of wonder. You realize that this moment—this beautiful, tender, miraculous moment—is one you will carry in your heart forever. It is a moment that will be etched into your soul, a moment that has already woven itself into the fabric of your life, changing it in the most extraordinary way. As you cradle your grandchild, you know that this is the beginning of something truly magical—a journey of love, joy, and unbreakable bonds that will last for a lifetime and beyond.

"A grandmother's love knows no distance."

Chapter Three

Navigating Boundaries.

Navigating the boundaries of your new role as a grandmother is a delicate and essential part of this beautiful journey. While the joy of welcoming a grandchild into the world is unparalleled, it also comes with the need to respect and honor the evolving dynamics within your family.

Your child is now stepping into the role of a parent, and the two of them will have their own approach, beliefs, and decisions about raising their child. This is their moment to shine, to learn, and to bond as a couple and a new family unit. As a grandmother, understanding and respecting this new chapter is crucial to fostering a healthy, supportive relationship that benefits everyone involved.

It's natural to want to share your experiences, to offer advice based on the many years you've spent raising your own children. However, it's important to remember that every generation has its own way of doing things, and what worked for you may not necessarily align with your child's vision of parenthood. The key is to offer guidance only when it is welcomed and to step back when it's not. This doesn't mean you are any less valuable in this new role; rather, it shows that you trust and respect your child's ability to parent, just as they will learn to trust in their instincts.

One of the most significant aspects of this chapter is recognizing that your child and their partner need time to bond with their baby as a family. It's a sacred period, one where they learn the rhythms of parenthood, find their confidence, and build their own unique bond with their newborn. **While it may be tempting to be there every moment, offering a bit of space can be one of the greatest gifts you can give them. It shows that you respect their need to create their own family memories and traditions, ones that they will cherish for a lifetime.**

Understanding their boundaries also requires a delicate balance of patience and communication. It's not always easy to know when to step in and when to step back, and that's okay. Open communication with your child and their partner is essential. Let them know that you are there to support them in any way they need but that you also understand the importance of their time as a new family. Ask them how they envision your role and what kind of help or involvement would be most beneficial to them. This collaborative approach not only strengthens your relationship but also helps to avoid any misunderstandings or feelings of overstepping.

Navigating these new waters means being flexible and adaptable. What might be helpful one day could be overwhelming the next. Being in tune with the needs of your child and grandchild requires a willingness to adjust your expectations and a readiness to support them in ways that truly make a difference. This flexibility will serve as a foundation for a harmonious relationship where everyone feels valued and heard.

It's also important to recognize that there will be moments of trial and error. You may unintentionally overstep, or perhaps feel excluded at times. These feelings are natural and part of the evolving family dynamic. The key is to approach each situation with empathy and understanding. Remember that your child is also learning how to balance their new role as a parent with their role as your child. Just as you are finding your footing as a grandmother, they are finding theirs as parents, and this process requires patience from all sides.

The delicate dance of family dynamics is about more than just respecting boundaries—it's about cultivating trust. Trust that your child will come to you when they need advice, trust that they will make the right decisions for their family, and trust that your bond with your grandchild will flourish in its own beautiful way. This trust is the bedrock of a strong, supportive family dynamic, one that allows each member to thrive in their respective roles.

One way to foster this trust is by celebrating your child's successes as a parent. Recognize and praise their efforts, even the small ones, and offer encouragement rather than unsolicited advice. When they feel confident and supported, they are more likely to turn to you for guidance and to involve you in meaningful ways. This positive reinforcement strengthens the family bond and reassures them that you are their ally, not a critic.

As a grandmother, it's also important to remember that your relationship with your grandchild will develop over time. It may not be instant, and that's okay. Building a strong bond comes from consistency, love, and being present in the ways that matter most. Whether it's a weekly visit, reading them a bedtime story over video chat, or simply being a reliable presence in their lives, these moments will lay the foundation for a lasting and loving relationship.

Respecting parental decisions is not about distancing yourself; it's about enhancing your role as a supportive and loving grandparent. It's about showing that you trust the parents' judgment and are there to support them in their journey. This respect will naturally lead to more open dialogue, more opportunities to connect with your grandchild, and more moments to share in the joy of watching them grow.

Navigating these family dynamics also involves recognizing your own needs and feelings. It's okay to feel a sense of loss as your role changes, but it's also an opportunity to redefine what it means to be a grandparent. It's a time to embrace the joys that come with this new chapter and to understand that love evolves and expands in ways that are beautiful and unexpected.

In the end, the journey of becoming a grandmother is about finding a balance between being there and stepping back, between offering guidance and letting go. It's about respecting the boundaries set by your child while also nurturing the deep, unbreakable bond that only a grandparent can have with their grandchild. It's a delicate dance, but one that, when done with love, patience, and respect, leads to a harmonious, joyful, and deeply fulfilling family dynamic that benefits everyone involved.

Grandmothers can no longer be defined by age, appearance, style or energy levels, we are just Mothers who were incredibly blessed and suddenly became GRAND!!

Chapter Four

Building Relationships with Adult Children without Overstepping.

Building strong relationships with your adult children as they navigate parenthood is a vital aspect of creating a loving, supportive family environment. As a grandmother, your role is unique and evolving; it involves balancing support and guidance with respect for their autonomy and decisions. The foundation of this relationship is built on trust, open communication, and the understanding that your role is to be a source of love and encouragement, not control. Approaching these relationships with care, empathy, and intention can create a harmonious atmosphere where everyone feels valued and supported.

Open communication is the cornerstone of any healthy relationship, especially when it comes to family dynamics that are shifting with the arrival of a new baby. Make it a point to express your love and pride in your adult children and their journey into parenthood. Acknowledge that becoming parents is a significant transition for them and that they will be finding their way, just as you did when you first became a parent. Let them know that you are available to listen, to share in their joys, and to offer support, but that you respect their independence in making decisions for their child.

One effective way to foster open communication is by asking questions rather than making assumptions. Instead of assuming that your help is needed or that your advice is wanted, ask how you can best support them. Questions like, "What would be most helpful for you right now?" or "Is there anything specific you'd like advice on?" show that you are there to assist in a way that respects their needs and preferences. This approach reduces the risk of unintentionally overstepping and helps to establish a partnership-like dynamic.

Being a supportive grandmother also means being a good listener. Sometimes, your children may just need to vent or share their experiences without wanting advice. Practice active listening by giving them your full attention, nodding, and providing affirmations without immediately jumping in with suggestions. Validate their feelings by saying things like, "That sounds really challenging" or "I can see why you'd feel that way." This helps to create a safe space where they feel heard and understood, rather than judged or instructed.

Offering support without overstepping involves understanding the difference between helping and controlling. It's easy to feel compelled to share your parenting wisdom, especially when you see them struggling with a situation you've faced before. However, unsolicited advice can sometimes feel like criticism, even when it comes from a place of love. Instead, try framing your advice as a shared experience: "When you were a baby, I found that this helped, but I know things are different now." This acknowledges your experience while also leaving room for them to decide what works best for their family.

Respecting their parenting choices is fundamental to building a strong relationship. Even if you disagree with a decision they make regarding your grandchild's diet, sleep schedule, or discipline methods, it's important to honor their role as parents. Offer your perspective if asked but avoid pushing your views. Remember, your goal is not to be right, but to support them in creating a happy, healthy environment for your grandchild. Trust in their ability to parent effectively and understand that they, too, are learning and growing in this new role.

Another key aspect of building a positive relationship is recognizing and respecting boundaries. Every family has different comfort levels when it comes to involvement, and these boundaries may evolve over time. Be attuned to verbal and non-verbal cues that may indicate when your presence is welcome and when they may need more space. It's okay to ask directly, "Am I around too much?" or "Would you like some time just the three of you?" This shows that you are considerate of their needs and are willing to adjust to ensure everyone feels comfortable.

Building relationships with the adult children of your child also means being mindful of your language. Use words that encourage and uplift rather than criticize or impose. Statements like, "You're doing such a great job" or "I'm so proud of how you're handling everything" can be very affirming. Avoid phrases that imply judgment or comparison, such as "I would never have done that" or "Back in my day, we did things differently." These comments can unintentionally create distance and defensiveness.

Celebrate their successes, no matter how small they may seem. Acknowledging milestones—whether it's the first time the baby sleeps through the night or their first successful outing as a family—helps to build their confidence as parents. Sharing in these joyful moments strengthens your bond and reinforces the idea that you are there to support them, not critique them. Showing genuine happiness for their achievements builds a positive, collaborative relationship.

One of the most powerful things you can offer your adult children is emotional support. Parenthood can be overwhelming and knowing that you are there to provide a listening ear, a shoulder to cry on, or even just a moment of relief can mean the world. Encourage them to take breaks and offer to babysit if they are comfortable with it, allowing them some time to recharge as a couple. This not only helps them maintain their own relationship but also shows that you are there to support the whole family unit.

Understanding that your adult children are navigating their own relationship dynamics as a couple is also crucial. Be mindful of how you interact with both partners, making sure to respect their decisions as a team. If one parent expresses a boundary or preference, avoid undermining them by going to the other parent. Consistency in respecting their united front will help to build trust and reinforce your role as a supportive presence in their lives.

It's also beneficial to maintain your own independence and life outside of being a grandmother. While it's wonderful to be involved, it's equally important to show that you have a fulfilling life of your own. This helps to set a healthy balance and prevents feelings of being overly dependent or too intertwined. Your adult children will likely appreciate knowing that you have your own hobbies, interests, and friendships that keep you engaged and happy.

Creating traditions and special rituals with your grandchildren can also strengthen your relationship with their parents. Whether it's a weekly story time, baking cookies together, or a special outing, these moments create cherished memories without infringing on the parents' time or traditions. Ensure that these activities are mutually agreed upon and align with the parents' values and routines.

Being a positive and dependable presence is more important than always having the right answer. Sometimes, just being there is enough. A simple text to check in, a quick call to say hello, or an offer to run an errand can mean a lot, especially during those early, exhausting months of parenthood. These small acts of kindness show that you are thinking of them and are available without demanding their time or attention.

It's also crucial to be mindful of your grandchild's needs and temperament. Respect the parents' guidelines on routines, diets, and sleep schedules, and be consistent in following them. This not only shows respect for their rules but also reinforces a sense of security and consistency for your grandchild, which is vital for their well-being.

Patience is another essential quality in building strong relationships with your adult children. Understand that there will be bumps along the way—moments of tension, misunderstanding, or disagreement. Approach these situations with calmness and a willingness to listen and learn. It's okay to apologize if you've overstepped or said something that didn't come out quite right. Humility and a genuine desire to maintain harmony go a long way in family relationships.

Acknowledging that each person's journey into parenthood is different is also key. Even among your own children, parenting styles may differ significantly. Respect these differences and avoid comparing one child's parenting choices to another's. Celebrate each family's unique approach and support them in the ways that best suit their individual needs.

Offering love and support extends beyond your grandchild—it involves caring for your adult children as they navigate their own challenges. Sometimes, this means stepping in with practical help, and other times, it means stepping back to allow them to figure things out on their own. Striking this balance requires constant adjustment and a sensitivity to their evolving needs.

Being open to change is also crucial. Family dynamics are fluid, and what works at one stage may not work at another. Stay flexible and be willing to adapt to new routines, schedules, and preferences as they arise. This openness to change fosters an environment of growth and positivity.

Finally, always remember that the love and effort you invest in these relationships will be returned tenfold. When your adult children see that you are committed to supporting them without infringing on their autonomy, they are more likely to welcome you into their lives and cherish the bond you share with your grandchild.

Chapter Five

The Joys of Babysitting.

Babysitting your grandchild is one of the sweetest joys of being a grandmother. There's something truly special about the moments when it's just you and your grandchild, free from the everyday rush, and the world seems to slow down just a little. You have the chance to be fully present, to experience the magic of their laughter, their curiosity, and their boundless energy. These moments are filled with simple joys—reading the same book over and over because they love it so much or playing hide and seek in the living room and hearing their delightful giggles when they find you (or when you pretend not to find them). It's a unique opportunity to build a deep, personal bond with your grandchild, one that is filled with love, trust, and a sense of wonder.

For grandmothers who are still in the workplace, juggling work and babysitting can feel like a balancing act, but it's also incredibly rewarding. There's something rejuvenating about switching gears from the responsibilities of work to the playful, carefree world of a child. While it requires careful planning and time management, it also brings a sense of purpose and fulfillment that's hard to match. Knowing that you are there for both your career and your family that you are still contributing and nurturing in meaningful ways, can be deeply satisfying. It requires flexibility and sometimes creativity to make it all work, but the rewards are worth every moment.

Being a grandmother as a caregiver means wearing many hats. On some days, you might find yourself building forts out of pillows, while on other days, you're helping with homework, or simply offering a comforting hug after a tough day. Each moment spent with your grandchild is a chance to teach, guide, and nurture. It's a role that allows you to be a mentor, a confidant, and a source of endless love. As a caregiver, you are not just looking after a child—you are shaping memories, building trust, and fostering a deep sense of belonging in your grandchild's heart.

For those grandmothers balancing work with caregiving, it's important to create a routine that supports both roles. Setting clear boundaries between work time and family time can help maintain a healthy balance. This might mean scheduling dedicated days or times for babysitting and finding moments within a busy work week to engage and bond with your grandchild. It might also involve setting up a home office that allows you to be flexible, stepping in and out of work mode as needed. Having a strong support system, both at work and at home, can make all the difference in managing this dual role.

When you're with your grandchild, it's a chance to immerse yourself fully in their world, to see life through their eyes. Every leaf becomes a treasure, every song an invitation to dance. You rediscover the joy in little things, the magic in everyday moments that, as adults, we often overlook. **As a grandmother, you have the wisdom to know that these moments are fleeting and precious, so you savor each one, holding** onto the laughter, the cuddles, and the joy that comes from simply being together.

The role of a grandmother as a caregiver also comes with a sense of fulfillment from knowing you are providing a safe, loving environment for your grandchild to grow and explore. Whether it's reading them a bedtime story, teaching them how to bake cookies, or simply sitting together and watching the clouds, these shared experiences help build a foundation of trust and love. It's not just about watching over them; it's about being there, fully present, providing a space where they feel secure, loved, and understood.

For those balancing work life and grandmother duties, it's essential to practice self-care. Juggling multiple responsibilities can be exhausting but taking time for yourself—whether it's a quiet cup of tea, a short walk, or a few minutes of meditation—can help replenish your energy and ensure that you can be fully present both at work and with your grandchild. It's about finding that balance where you can give your best in all aspects of your life without feeling overwhelmed.

Being a grandmother in a caregiving role also allows you to be creative and resourceful. You learn to adapt to the ever-changing needs of a growing child and to find ways to turn everyday activities into fun, learning experiences. Cooking becomes a lesson in measuring and counting; a walk in the park turns into an adventure of discovering leaves and insects. Your grandchild looks to you for guidance and inspiration, and in turn, you find new ways to keep them engaged, learning, and exploring the world around them.

There's also the joy of seeing your grandchild's personality develop, their preferences and quirks coming to life in the little choices they make. It's in the way they insist on wearing their favorite hat everywhere or how they giggle at the same silly joke every time. These little traits and habits are glimpses into who they are becoming, and as a grandmother, you get a front-row seat to this beautiful unfolding. It's a privilege to watch them grow, to be there for the milestones and the moments in between.

As a caregiver, your relationship with your grandchild is based on a foundation of trust and unconditional love. They know that when they're with you, they are safe, cherished, and free to be themselves. This trust creates an environment where they can express themselves, explore their feelings, and learn new things with confidence. It's a bond that grows stronger with each shared story, each comforting hug, and each moment of laughter.

One of the great joys of babysitting as a grandmother is the opportunity to pass down family traditions and stories. You become the keeper of family history, sharing tales from the past that connect your grandchild to their roots. Whether it's a story about their parent as a child or a cherished recipe passed down through generations, these moments of sharing help instill a sense of belonging and continuity, anchoring them in a family narrative that is rich and meaningful.

Managing both work and babysitting duties requires good communication with your adult children. Understanding their needs and expectations and setting clear agreements can help prevent misunderstandings and ensure that everyone is on the same page. It's about working together to create a balance that supports the child's well-being while respecting everyone's time and commitments. Being flexible and open to adjustments as needed will help keep this dynamic healthy and positive.

There's a unique joy in the quiet moments, too—those times when your grandchild falls asleep in your arms, and you're left with the stillness of the room and the rhythmic sound of their breathing. In these moments, you feel the profound love and responsibility of being a grandmother, of nurturing this little life that is so deeply connected to your own. It's a feeling of completeness, a sense of contentment that comes from knowing you are playing a vital role in their life.

For grandmothers balancing work and caregiving, creating a supportive network is crucial. This network might include friends, family, and colleagues who understand the dual roles you are managing. Whether it's arranging for backup childcare on busy workdays or sharing tips and experiences with other grandmothers, having a community can make the journey more manageable and enjoyable.

In the end, the joy of babysitting your grandchild, whether you are juggling a career or are fully dedicated to your role as a grandmother, is a joy that is deeply enriching. It's about embracing the chaos, the laughter, and the love that comes with spending time with a child who sees the world with fresh eyes. It's about knowing that the time you invest now will blossom into a relationship filled with trust, love, and endless memories that both you and your grandchild will cherish for a lifetime.

When the child you love
has a child you love with all that is
within you, only then
will you know just how grand being a
grandparent truly is."

Chapter Six

Sharing Wisdom. Passing Down Family Stories, Teaching Traditional Skills.

Sharing wisdom with your grandchildren is one of the most rewarding aspects of being a grandmother. It's an opportunity to pass down the life lessons you've learned, the values you've cherished, and the insights that have shaped you. Unlike the rushed days of parenting, grandparenthood often provides a calmer, more reflective space to share these precious gems of wisdom. Whether it's about kindness, resilience, or the importance of staying true to oneself, these lessons often resonate more deeply when shared through the loving relationship of a grandparent and grandchild. As you tell them stories or give advice, you are not just teaching; you are weaving a rich tapestry of understanding and connection between generations.

Family stories are powerful tools for imparting wisdom. They carry with them the essence of who we are and where we come from, creating a sense of continuity and belonging. When you share stories about your own childhood, or recount tales of their parents when they were young, you are giving your grandchildren a window into their heritage. These stories help them understand their roots and see themselves as part of something larger than the here and now. A story about a family member's courage, kindness, or even their mistakes, can provide valuable lessons about character, resilience, and growth.

Passing down family stories also creates an emotional bridge between generations. When your grandchildren hear about their great-grandparents' adventures, sacrifices, and dreams, they gain a deeper appreciation for their family history. They learn to value the people who came before them and the contributions that shaped their lives. These stories are not just about the past; they help them navigate their present and future, armed with the wisdom of those who have walked similar paths. By sharing these stories, you are helping to root them in a legacy of love, strength, and perseverance.

Teaching traditional skills is another beautiful way to pass on wisdom. Whether it's baking a family recipe, knitting a scarf, or planting a garden, these skills carry with them the essence of generations past. When you teach a grandchild how to make a dish that has been passed down through the family, you are not just sharing a recipe; you are sharing a piece of your history, a connection to those who came before you. These moments spent together in the kitchen or garden become memories in themselves, ones that they will carry forward and possibly pass on to their own children one day.

Traditional skills are also a way to teach practical lessons about patience, creativity, and perseverance. As your grandchild learns how to knead dough, tend to plants, or sew a button, they also learn the value of taking time to do something well, the joy of creating with their hands, and the satisfaction of seeing a project through to the end.

Chapter Seven

If the Unthinkable happens.
The Not So Good Parts.

I felt it was important to at least share some of the not so good parts of being a grandparent.

When families are together and happy, and everything is working out life is good.

But heaven forbid if divorce happens in your child's life, and you are the mother-in-law (aka grandmother) and your son wants a divorce or divorces your daughter in law – things can go bad really fast.

Learn from me – stay out of the drama – it causes so much pain even years down the road – some women are amazing and put their children first, but there are others who put revenge first, to the detriment of the child.

Children Should Not Be Pawns

Since my granddaughter came into this world, we have spent so much time in each others company. We have done so much together - we created a lot, a lot of memories. She stole my heart, and I fell hopelessly in love with her.

We were like two peas in a pod; everyone thought she was my daughter. We created so many memories, spending a weekend at a bed and breakfast, having high tea at the fancy tea house, going to the spa together, getting our nails done, and going on adventures to the teddy bear museum. – these were just some of the things we did together. She helped me with my presentations, dressed up in fancy clothing, and accompanied me to my networking and business events...

All that changed when her parents filed for divorce.

I knew divorce could be a messy procedure, but I never dreamed of how much my little angel would be harmed in the process of her parents separating. I was even more shocked to see the other side of my daughter-in-law. The worst thing of all: I was horror struck by how this affected my beloved granddaughter.

I tried to make it easy on her, but the constant fighting; the vicious verbal attacks from her mother that she overheard time and time again were slowly doing irrevocable damage to her gentle soul. Every time I saw her, she whispers sweet things into my ear, telling me she loves me, misses our adventures together, and how she wants to come spend time with me, like we used to.

These little whispers cover the hurt that she feels deep down inside, and I can see her acting out when she tells her mother she hates her. She doesn't feel that way, but that is the only way that she has to express her feelings. When her mother refuses to let her father see the child, it hurts my little angel more than anyone knows. "*I miss daddy so much Nanni.*" These are the words she tells me, when her mother is out of earshot.

I found that:

- 43% of children in the U.S. today live without their fathers.

- 50% of children will see their parents' divorce, and almost half will see a second divorce as well.

- 10% of children in the country experience more than three parental breakups.

If these children go through something similar to what my granddaughter is going through, I can only imagine how their lives are affected by divorce.

Sometimes the only peace for these little children is their grandparents, and if that is simultaneously taken away, the damage to a child could be horrendous.

During a storm, when the winds of life tear at the fabric of a family, children often become the silent victims of their parents' struggles. Divorce, with all its complexity and emotional weight, can be a tumultuous experience, especially for the youngest hearts. In these difficult times, grandmothers can become a powerful refuge for children, offering a haven of love, stability, and protection from the emotional turbulence surrounding them.

When parents decide to divorce, it is essential to remember that the children are not divorcing their parents. They are not the ones who chose this path, yet they often bear the brunt of the emotional fallout. As parents untangle their lives, children can feel lost in the shuffle, caught between the people they love the most. This is where the role of a grandmother becomes not just important but truly irreplaceable.

A grandmother, with her years of wisdom and experience, can be a calming presence in a child's life. She stands as a symbol of unconditional love, a reminder that not everything in their world is falling apart. While their parents may be facing difficult emotions, arguments, and legal battles, a grandmother's love remains steady and unwavering. Her home, whether physical or emotional, becomes a place of shelter, a safe space where a child can find solace, stability, and reassurance.

Grandmothers know the power of love that transcends the complexities of adult conflict. They understand that children should never become pawns in their parents' battle, that their emotional well-being should be prioritized above all else.

Grandmothers, through their nurturing and compassionate nature, can protect the child from the emotional harm that comes with feeling torn between two parents. They offer not just a physical space to escape the stress but an emotional one, where the child is free to express their feelings without fear of judgment or pressure.

The presence of a grandmother can ease a child's confusion, helping them navigate the painful realities of divorce. Through gentle conversations and consistent reassurance, a grandmother can remind the child that even though their family dynamics are changing, the love from both parents remains constant. In her presence, children can find peace in knowing they are not alone in their pain. They have a champion, someone who will stand by their side through the storm.

A grandmother's home can be a place where the rules of the battle don't apply, where the child doesn't have to choose sides or feel the weight of divided loyalties. In this space, love is simple, pure, and unconditional. Grandmothers provide more than just physical shelter; they offer emotional shelter. They listen when the child needs to talk, hug when words fail, and offer simple joys—a favorite meal, a bedtime story, or a cozy spot on the couch—that remind the child that life is still filled with love.

Divorce is hard, but for the children involved, it doesn't have to leave scars that last a lifetime. Grandmothers, with their loving hearts, can be the steady, warm embrace that keeps the child anchored when everything else seems to be falling apart. Their wisdom, patience, and unwavering love can protect a child from the emotional damage that divorce can inflict, helping them emerge from the storm with their spirit intact. In a grandmother's arms, a child finds shelter, security, and the comfort of knowing that no matter what happens, they are deeply loved.

And one final note to all grandmothers, stay out of it – let them find their way, even if it gets nasty – don't get involved – your only job is to be there for your grandchildren.

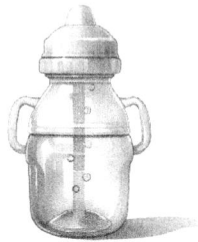

"A grandmother is a sunbeam, warming her family with love that shines brighter with each grandchild's touch."

Chapter Eight
The Perfect Gifts.

Choosing the perfect gift for your grandchild is a delightful opportunity to express your love and thoughtfulness. As a grandmother, you want each present to be a token of your affection and a cherished memory. The perfect gift goes beyond just the excitement of unwrapping it; it holds meaning, intention, and a piece of your heart. It could be something that inspires their imagination, nurtures their growth, or even connects them to family traditions. The key is to choose gifts that will not only bring immediate joy but also have a lasting impact on their lives, reflecting your unique bond with them.

When selecting a meaningful present, it's essential to consider the personality and interests of your grandchild. Think about what makes them smile, what captures their curiosity, and what they love to talk about. Are they fascinated by dinosaurs, or do they have a passion for drawing and painting? Perhaps they love building things with their hands or have an insatiable love for stories and books. Choosing gifts that align with their interests not only shows that you pay attention to their likes but also encourages them to pursue their passions.

Striking a balance between fun and practicality is another important consideration. A perfect gift doesn't have to be purely educational or entirely entertaining; it can be a blend of both. For example, a beautifully illustrated book can be fun to read while also encouraging a love for literature and expanding their vocabulary. Similarly, a set of colorful building blocks can offer hours of imaginative play while simultaneously enhancing their fine motor skills and problem-solving abilities. By combining elements of fun and learning, you give them a gift that delights and benefits them at the same time.

Sentimental gifts often hold a special place in a grandchild's heart. These could be heirlooms passed down through generations, like a locket with a family picture, a handmade quilt, or a cherished book you read to their parent when they were young. Such gifts carry stories and emotions that connect them to their roots and family heritage. These presents not only offer comfort but also serve as a bridge between the past and the present, providing them with a sense of belonging and identity.

Personalized gifts can also be incredibly meaningful. A custom storybook where your grandchild is the hero of the tale, a name-engraved wooden puzzle, or a piece of jewelry with their birthstone can make them feel extra special. These personalized presents show that you went the extra mile to create something uniquely theirs, something that they can look back on fondly as a reminder of their special bond with you.

Practical gifts are also a wonderful option, especially when they cater to the child's everyday needs in a thoughtful way. Items like a cozy blanket for bedtime, a stylish backpack for school, or a sturdy pair of rain boots for outdoor adventures are practical yet heartfelt. These gifts become a part of their daily life, offering comfort and utility while reminding them of your care and thoughtfulness every time they use them.

Sometimes, the best gifts are experiences rather than physical objects. Consider gifting your grandchild an experience that you can share together, like a day at the zoo, tickets to a children's theater performance, or a special baking day at home where you can teach them a family recipe. These experiences not only create lasting memories but also provide an opportunity for bonding, learning, and sharing moments that they will treasure for years to come.

Creative gifts that inspire your grandchild's imagination and creativity are always a great choice. Art supplies, musical instruments, or a DIY science kit can provide endless hours of fun while encouraging them to explore their talents and interests. By giving them tools to create and discover, you are nurturing their sense of curiosity and self-expression, which are invaluable gifts in their own right.

Educational gifts that promote learning in a fun way are also perfect. Puzzles, interactive globes, STEM toys, or subscription boxes that deliver science or craft kits every month can keep them engaged and excited about learning new things. These types of gifts stimulate their minds and foster a love for discovery and exploration, which can greatly benefit their development.

In the end, the perfect gift for your grandchild is one that reflects your love, thoughtfulness, and understanding of who they are. It's a gift that balances fun and practicality, offers a meaningful connection, and provides joy both in the present and for years to come. Whether it's a treasured heirloom, a personalized keepsake, a practical everyday item, a creative tool, or an unforgettable experience, the best gifts come from the heart. And as a grandmother, the most valuable gift you give is your time, love, and the memories you create together, making every gift you choose a cherished part of your grandchild's life.

Cool Gift Ideas for Grandchildren:

1. **Personalized Storybook**: Where they are the main character.

2. **Building Blocks or LEGO Set**: For creativity and motor skills.

3. **Art Supplies Kit**: Encourage their creative side with paints, markers, and canvases.

4. **Heirloom Jewelry**: A locket with a family photo or a charm bracelet.

5. **Experience Day**: A zoo visit, theater tickets, or a cooking day together.

6. **Custom Puzzle with Their Name**: Fun and personal.

7. **Educational Subscription Box**: Monthly science, reading, or craft kits.

8. **Children's Globe or Map**: To learn about the world.

9. **Classic Book Set**: Books you loved and want to share with them.

10. **Interactive STEM Toy**: For learning science, technology, engineering, and math.

11. **Musical Instrument**: A beginner's piano, ukulele, or drum set.

12. **Gardening Kit**: Tools and seeds for a small vegetable or flower garden.

13. **Custom-made Blanket**: With their favorite colors or characters.

14. **Rain Boots and Jacket Set**: For jumping in puddles.

15. **Personalized Backpack**: For school or travel.

16. **Memory Jar**: Filled with notes of shared memories and future plans.

17. **Adventure Kit**: Binoculars, a compass, and a journal for exploring.

18. **Scrapbook Kit**: For creating and keeping family memories.

19. **Baking Kit**: Child-friendly tools and a recipe book.

20. **Family Board Games**: Fun for the whole family to play together.

These gifts are sure to delight and leave a lasting impression on your grandchild, blending thoughtfulness, fun, and a touch of practicality.

"To be called 'grandmother' is to be entrusted with the most ancient of honors—raising the light of love for generations to follow."

Chapter Nine

Long-Distance Grand mothering.

For grandmothers who live far away from their grandchildren, staying connected can be a challenge, but with today's technology, it's easier than ever to bridge the distance and build a meaningful relationship. Virtual tools and creative planning can bring you closer to your grandchild, allowing you to be present in their lives despite the miles between you. Whether it's through video calls, digital storytelling, or planning exciting adventures for when you visit, there are many ways to make your bond strong and vibrant.

Video calls have become one of the most popular ways for grandparents to stay in touch with their grandchildren. Platforms like Zoom, FaceTime, or Skype offer the opportunity for face-to-face interactions, even when you're continents apart. Regularly scheduled video calls, perhaps once a week or every other week, can create a sense of routine and anticipation for both you and your grandchild. During these calls, you can read stories, share jokes, sing songs, or even play simple games that keep the interaction lively and engaging

Beyond just chatting, video calls can be a wonderful way to participate in daily activities from afar. You can help them with their homework, watch them perform their new dance routine, or even virtually join them for breakfast or dinner. Sharing these everyday moments helps to maintain a sense of closeness and normalcy, making your presence a natural part of their life, even if it is through a screen.

Another fantastic way to stay connected is through digital storytelling. There are apps and websites that allow you to record yourself reading stories or telling tales, which your grandchild can listen to anytime they want. This creates a sense of intimacy, as they hear your voice narrating bedtime stories, just as if you were there. You can also create and share personalized stories featuring them as the hero, sparking their imagination and making them feel incredibly special.

Interactive games that can be played over the internet, like digital board games or drawing apps, provide another fun way to connect. Whether it's a classic game of checkers or a creative app that lets you draw and guess each other's doodles, these activities allow you to share laughter and joy despite the physical distance. Playing games together fosters a sense of camaraderie and closeness that can often mirror the fun of being together in person.

Technology also allows for collaborative projects that can be done over long distances. For example, you could work on a shared digital scrapbook where both of you add photos, drawings, and stories. Or, you could cook a recipe together over a video call, each in your own kitchen, and compare the results. These activities create shared experiences and memories that strengthen your bond and give you both something to look forward to.

Another creative way to stay connected is by creating a "virtual adventure club" with your grandchild. Plan themed video calls where you explore different countries, learn about their cultures, and even try to cook traditional dishes together. This not only keeps your relationship engaging and educational but also adds a unique and fun twist to your virtual meetings. It's like going on a little adventure together without leaving your home.

Letters may seem old-fashioned but pairing them with modern technology can be very special. Writing letters or postcards, and then discussing them over a video call, creates a multi-dimensional form of communication that can be deeply meaningful. Your grandchild can keep your letters and look back on them whenever they miss you, creating a tangible connection that complements the digital one.

Planning adventure visits and vacations is another exciting way to stay connected. These plans can become something that you both look forward to, and the anticipation itself can be a fun part of the experience. You can brainstorm ideas together over video calls or messaging apps—whether it's a trip to a nearby zoo, a day at the beach, or even a themed staycation. Letting your grandchild have a say in the planning makes them feel involved and excited about the time you will spend together.

When planning these visits, consider creating a "Grandma Adventure Book" filled with potential trips and activities. This book can be shared digitally, allowing both you and your grandchild to add ideas, comments, and plans. Whether it's visiting a new museum, going on a treasure hunt in the local park, or making homemade ice cream, this book becomes a collaborative project that keeps you both engaged.

For vacations, consider planning a longer, more involved trip that allows you to spend quality time together. This could be a week-long visit to a favorite location, such as a beach house, a national park, or a theme park. With tools like Google Earth or interactive maps, you can "travel" together virtually beforehand, choosing destinations, learning about the area, and planning your itinerary.

Beyond planning adventures, consider organizing virtual events like "Grandma's Cooking Show" where you and your grandchild cook a simple recipe together over video. You can teach them a traditional family recipe, share stories about its origins, and enjoy the fun (and sometimes messy) process together. These virtual cooking sessions can become cherished memories and provide a sense of tradition.

Technology also offers the chance to send digital gifts and surprises. Surprise your grandchild with a digital gift card for an online bookstore, a fun app, or a subscription to a monthly activity box that you can explore together over video calls. Small surprises like these can show them that you are thinking of them, even from afar.

Creating a shared playlist of favorite songs, stories, or even bedtime lullabies is another wonderful way to stay connected. Platforms like Spotify or Apple Music allow you to build and share playlists, creating a soundtrack of your relationship. Listening to the same songs or stories creates a sense of unity, even when you are miles apart.

Virtual book clubs are another engaging idea. Choose a book to read together and set a time to discuss it over video calls. This not only encourages reading but also provides an opportunity for deep conversations and bonding over shared interests. It's a simple but effective way to stay intellectually and emotionally connected.

You can also create a shared calendar that includes not only your planned video calls but also special dates like birthdays, holidays, and any fun events you plan to virtually attend together. This helps in building anticipation and keeping track of all the exciting things you'll be doing together, ensuring that the connection stays strong and consistent.

For grandmothers who want to add an educational twist, consider creating a "Learning with Grandma" series of video calls. You can teach them simple things like how to plant seeds, identify birds, or even some basic science experiments. Learning together not only fosters curiosity but also provides valuable bonding time.

Consider creating a shared "Adventure Jar" where you both contribute ideas for future activities. This jar can be digital (like a shared document) or physical (where you each add ideas during visits). Pulling out a new idea for each call or visit adds an element of surprise and excitement.

Planning for the holidays when you're apart is another meaningful way to stay connected. You can make matching decorations, send care packages filled with holiday goodies, and plan virtual celebrations together. Making the distance seem less daunting by participating in these holiday traditions adds warmth and continuity to your relationship.

Lastly, don't forget the power of consistency. Regularly scheduled calls, surprise messages, and thoughtful activities all build a strong foundation of love and connection. Your grandchild will come to treasure these moments and look forward to every interaction, knowing that their grandmother is always just a call or a message away.

Tips for Staying Connected as a Long-Distance Grandmother:

1. **Schedule Regular Video Calls**: Set up weekly or bi-weekly video chats.
2. **Create a Virtual Adventure Club**: Explore new places together online.
3. **Digital Storytelling**: Record yourself reading their favorite stories.
4. **Interactive Online Games**: Play games like digital chess or drawing apps together.
5. **Collaborative Projects**: Create digital scrapbooks or photo albums together.
6. **Plan Adventure Visits**: Discuss future visits and trips, making them a joint effort.
7. **Write Letters or Postcards**: Compliment digital communication with handwritten notes.
8. **Send Digital Gifts and Surprises**: Like e-books, apps, or subscriptions.
9. **Virtual Cooking Classes**: Share family recipes over video calls.
10. **Shared Playlists**: Curate music or story playlists to listen to together.
11. **Virtual Book Club**: Choose and read books together, discussing them later.
12. **Create a Shared Calendar**: Keep track of virtual and physical events.
13. **Host Virtual Events**: Like a "Grandma's Talent Show" or a craft day.
14. **Teach Them Something New**: From knitting to gardening, host learning sessions.

15. **Create an Adventure Jar**: Share and draw activity ideas for each call or visit.
16. **Plan Virtual Holidays Together**: Make decorations or share holiday traditions.
17. **Share Virtual Tours**: Visit museums, zoos, or historical sites online together.
18. **Use Interactive Learning Apps**: Co-play educational games or lessons.
19. **Record Video Messages**: Send them as surprises when they least expect it.
20. **Stay Consistent**: Regular contact is key to maintaining a strong bond.

These tips can help grandmothers remain an integral part of their grandchildren's lives, nurturing a close and loving relationship despite the distance.

"A grandmother is a little bit parent, a little bit teacher, and a little bit best friend"

Chapter Ten

Grandmother's Health and Self-Care.

Taking care of oneself is crucial for grandmothers who want to be vibrant, active, and present in their grandchildren's lives. **Self-care is not a luxury but a necessity, especially for those who cherish spending quality time with their grandchildren and want to be there for many years to come.** By prioritizing self-care, grandmothers ensure they have the energy, strength, and emotional resilience needed to keep up with their grandchildren's boundless enthusiasm and to be the best version of themselves.

Staying physically active is one of the most important aspects of self-care for grandmothers. Regular exercise not only helps to maintain strength and flexibility but also boosts energy levels and mood. Activities like walking, swimming, yoga, or even dancing can be fun and accessible ways to stay fit. Incorporating physical activity into daily routines keeps the body strong and reduces the risk of age-related ailments. Plus, it sets a great example for grandchildren, teaching them the importance of staying active from an early age

Eating healthy is another fundamental component of self-care. A balanced diet rich in fruits, vegetables, lean proteins, and whole grains provides the nutrients needed for energy, bone health, and overall well-being. Staying hydrated and reducing sugar and processed food intake can also make a significant difference in how one feels. By choosing nutritious foods, grandmothers can maintain a healthy weight, prevent chronic diseases, and have the stamina to play, run, and explore with their grandchildren.

Managing stress is equally essential for grandmothers who want to be fully present and engaged with their families. Life can be hectic, and balancing various responsibilities—whether it's work, family, or personal commitments—can be overwhelming. Learning stress management techniques such as mindfulness, meditation, or deep breathing exercises can help calm the mind and reduce anxiety. By taking a few minutes each day to breathe deeply and relax, grandmothers can cultivate inner peace, which radiates outward and positively impacts those around them.

Another vital aspect of self-care is ensuring adequate sleep. Quality sleep is critical for physical health, mental clarity, and emotional well-being. It allows the body to repair, restore, and recharge for the day ahead. A well-rested grandmother is more likely to have the patience and energy needed to keep up with young children. Creating a calming bedtime routine, limiting screen time before bed, and keeping a regular sleep schedule can all contribute to better sleep quality and overall health.

Taking time for oneself is an often overlooked but essential part of being a healthy and happy grandmother. Engaging in activities that bring joy and relaxation—such as gardening, reading, painting, or simply taking a leisurely walk—can be incredibly rejuvenating. These moments of personal time help grandmothers recharge and maintain their sense of identity outside of their caregiving role. When grandmothers are happy and fulfilled, they are better equipped to share that joy and positivity with their grandchildren.

Building a support network is another crucial component of self-care. Staying connected with friends, joining clubs or groups, and maintaining a social life helps combat loneliness and promotes emotional well-being. Whether it's a book club, a fitness class, or just a group of friends who meet for coffee, having a community provides a sense of belonging and support. A strong social network is vital for emotional health, and it offers a space to share experiences, seek advice, and laugh together.

Regular medical check-ups and preventive care are also critical for grandmothers who want to remain healthy and active. Keeping up with doctor visits, screenings, and vaccinations ensures that any potential health issues are detected early and managed effectively. Taking care of one's health proactively allows grandmothers to focus on enjoying their time with their grandchildren rather than worrying about potential health concerns.

Grandmothers should also consider incorporating activities that promote mental agility and cognitive health. Engaging in puzzles, learning new skills, playing strategy games, or even taking classes can help keep the mind sharp and active. Cognitive health is crucial for maintaining a good quality of life and being able to engage fully with grandchildren, whether that's helping with homework, telling stories, or playing games that require quick thinking.

Balancing the time spent with grandchildren and time for personal hobbies is key to a well-rounded life. While being a hands-on grandmother is incredibly rewarding, it's also essential to nurture one's passions and interests. By pursuing hobbies and personal goals, grandmothers show their grandchildren the importance of lifelong learning and following one's passions, setting a positive example for them to emulate.

It's also important for grandmothers to set boundaries to protect their time and energy. While it can be tempting to always be available for family, setting healthy boundaries ensures that there is time for self-care and rest. Communicating openly with family members about needs and limits can help create a balanced, respectful relationship that benefits everyone.

Finding time for mindfulness and reflection can help grandmothers stay grounded and focused. Practices like journaling, meditating, or simply spending quiet time in nature can help clear the mind, reduce stress, and promote emotional resilience. Mindfulness encourages being present in the moment, which can deepen the connection between grandmothers and their grandchildren during their time together.

Staying hydrated is another simple yet crucial aspect of self-care. Drinking enough water throughout the day helps maintain energy levels, supports cognitive function, and promotes overall health. Simple habits like carrying a reusable water bottle or drinking a glass of water with each meal can make a big difference.

Engaging in positive self-talk and maintaining a healthy mindset is vital for a happy, balanced life. Reminding oneself of strengths, practicing gratitude, and focusing on positive aspects of life can improve mental and emotional well-being. A positive mindset is contagious, and grandchildren will benefit from being around a grandmother who radiates optimism and joy.

Ultimately, a happy, healthy grandmother is the best gift to any grandchild. By taking care of themselves—through physical activity, healthy eating, stress management, social engagement, and time for personal growth—grandmothers can ensure they are strong, vibrant, and ready to make the most of every moment with their grandchildren. This commitment to self-care not only benefits them but also enhances the quality of the time they spend with their loved ones, creating lasting memories filled with love, laughter, and joy.

My hugs and kisses will always be bigger
and warmer than all the stuffed
toys you will ever have.

Chapter Eleven
Educating Yourself.

Staying educated on what is happening in the world is an essential part of being a well-rounded and informed grandmother. In a rapidly changing world, it's important to keep up with current events, societal trends, and technological advancements to better understand the environment in which your grandchildren are growing up. Being informed allows you to engage in meaningful conversations with them as they grow older and become more aware of the world around them. It also helps you provide guidance and wisdom rooted in current realities, which is invaluable for helping them navigate the complexities of today's society.

Keeping up-to-date with modern parenting practices is equally crucial. Parenting styles and philosophies have evolved significantly over the years, with new research and insights reshaping the way parents raise their children. Understanding these changes allows you to offer support that aligns with the values and methods that your grandchildren's parents are using. This doesn't mean abandoning your own tried-and-true wisdom; rather, it means blending it with new ideas and approaches. This can create a balanced, harmonious relationship with your children and grandchildren, where you offer relevant advice and avoid potential conflicts over outdated practices.

Learning new skills and hobbies is another fantastic way to stay active, engaged, and inspirational. Grandchildren often look up to their grandparents and see them as role models. By showing them that learning is a lifelong journey, and that age is no barrier to picking up new skills, you inspire them to cultivate a growth mindset. Whether it's learning a new language, mastering a musical instrument, taking up digital photography, or exploring gardening, these new endeavors not only enrich your own life but also serve as a testament to your adaptability and enthusiasm for learning.

Staying educated also involves embracing technology. From smartphones to social media to smart home devices, the digital world is an integral part of your grandchildren's lives. By becoming tech-savvy, you not only make it easier to stay connected with them, especially if you live far away, but you also show them that age is no barrier to learning and mastering new tools. You can participate in their digital experiences, understand the platforms they use, and even share in their digital hobbies, like gaming or digital storytelling, creating unique and memorable bonding moments.

Being aware of educational trends and resources can also help you guide your grandchildren effectively. Whether they are learning coding in school, being taught through hands-on STEM activities, or navigating online learning platforms, understanding these tools and methods allows you to engage more deeply with their education. You can offer additional resources, suggest helpful apps, or even learn alongside them, turning education into a shared, fun experience. Your involvement shows them that learning is valuable and can be a family activity.

Understanding current societal issues, such as climate change, diversity, inclusion, and mental health, also positions you as a more informed and empathetic guide. Today's youth are growing up in a world that is more socially conscious and globally connected than ever before. By staying informed on these topics, you can have meaningful discussions with your grandchildren and help them navigate their own thoughts and feelings about these issues. You can also share your values and experiences while being open to new perspectives, fostering an environment of mutual respect and learning.

Taking courses, attending workshops, or joining community groups can also help you stay engaged and educated. Many communities offer adult education classes, and there are countless online resources available for free or at a low cost. Whether it's a course on modern parenting, a workshop on digital literacy, or a club for new hobbies like painting or gardening, these experiences not only keep your mind active but also expand your social network. Engaging with peers who share similar interests provides a supportive environment for learning and growth.

Your enthusiasm for learning and staying updated also encourages your grandchildren to adopt similar habits. When they see you exploring new things, asking questions, and challenging yourself, they learn the value of curiosity and lifelong learning. They see that age is no obstacle to growth and that their grandmother is not only a loving figure but also a dynamic, evolving individual. This inspires them to be proactive in their own learning journeys and to remain open-minded about the world around them.

Moreover, embracing new hobbies and skills can create opportunities for intergenerational bonding. If you learn to play a new musical instrument, for instance, you can teach them, or you can both learn together. If you take up digital photography, you can go on photo walks and capture memories together. These shared experiences build stronger relationships, create lasting memories, and enrich both of your lives. They see you not just as a grandparent but as a companion in their adventures.

Ultimately, staying educated, adaptable, and engaged in new learning makes you a more inspirational figure in your grandchildren's lives. You show them that life is about continuous growth, that curiosity has no age limit, and that wisdom is a blend of old and new. By being informed, learning new skills, embracing modern technology, and understanding today's parenting dynamics, you not only remain relevant but also become a trusted guide and role model for them. Your commitment to growth and education leaves a lasting legacy that will impact them for years to come.

When they placed you in my arms you slipped into my heart. I never knew how much a person could love until I became a grandmother.

Chapter Twelve
Leaving a Legacy.

Staying educated on what is happening in the world is an essential part of being a well-rounded and informed grandmother. In a rapidly changing world, it's important to keep up with current events, societal trends, and technological advancements to better understand the environment in which your grandchildren are growing up. Being informed allows you to engage in meaningful conversations with them as they grow older and become more aware of the world around them. It also helps you provide guidance and wisdom rooted in current realities, which is invaluable for helping them navigate the complexities of today's society.

Keeping up to date with modern parenting practices is equally crucial. Parenting styles and philosophies have evolved significantly over the years, with new research and insights reshaping the way parents raise their children. Understanding these changes allows you to offer support that aligns with the values and methods that your grandchildren's parents are using. This doesn't mean abandoning your own tried-and-true wisdom; rather, it means blending it with new ideas and approaches. This can create a balanced, harmonious relationship with your children and grandchildren, where you offer relevant advice and avoid potential conflicts over outdated practices.

Learning new skills and hobbies is another fantastic way to stay active, engaged, and inspirational. Grandchildren often look up to their grandparents and see them as role models. By showing them that learning is a lifelong journey and that age is no barrier to picking up new skills, you inspire them to cultivate a growth mindset. Whether it's learning a new language, mastering a musical instrument, taking up digital photography, or exploring gardening, these new endeavors not only enrich your own life but also serve as a testament to your adaptability and enthusiasm for learning.

Staying educated also involves embracing technology. From smartphones to social media to smart home devices, the digital world is an integral part of your grandchildren's lives. By becoming tech-savvy, you not only make it easier to stay connected with them, especially if you live far away, but you also show them that age is no barrier to learning and mastering new tools. You can participate in their digital experiences, understand the platforms they use, and even share in their digital hobbies, like gaming or digital storytelling, creating unique and memorable bonding moments.

Being aware of educational trends and resources can also help you guide your grandchildren effectively. Whether they are learning coding in school, being taught through hands-on STEM activities, or navigating online learning platforms, understanding these tools and methods allows you to engage more deeply with their education. You can offer additional resources, suggest helpful apps, or even learn alongside them, turning education into a shared, fun experience. Your involvement shows them that learning is valuable and can be a family activity.

Understanding current societal issues, such as climate change, diversity, inclusion, and mental health, also positions you as a more informed and empathetic guide. Today's youth are growing up in a world that is more socially conscious and globally connected than ever before. By staying informed on these topics, you can have meaningful discussions with your grandchildren and help them navigate their own thoughts and feelings about these issues. You can also share your values and experiences while being open to new perspectives, fostering an environment of mutual respect and learning.

Taking courses, attending workshops, or joining community groups can also help you stay engaged and educated. Many communities offer adult education classes, and there are countless online resources available for free or at a low cost. Whether it's a course on modern parenting, a workshop on digital literacy, or a club for new hobbies like painting or gardening, these experiences not only keep your mind active but also expand your social network. Engaging with peers who share similar interests provides a supportive environment for learning and growth.

Your enthusiasm for learning and staying updated also encourages your grandchildren to adopt similar habits. When they see you exploring new things, asking questions, and challenging yourself, they learn the value of curiosity and lifelong learning. They see that age is no obstacle to growth and that their grandmother is not only a loving figure but also a dynamic, evolving individual. This inspires them to be proactive in their own learning journeys and to remain open-minded about the world around them.

Moreover, embracing new hobbies and skills can create opportunities for intergenerational bonding. If you learn to play a new musical instrument, for instance, you can teach them, or you can both learn together. If you take up digital photography, you can go on photo walks and capture memories together. These shared experiences build stronger relationships, create lasting memories, and enrich both of your lives. They see you not just as a grandparent but as a companion in their adventures.

Ultimately, staying educated, adaptable, and engaged in new learning makes you a more inspirational figure in your grandchildren's lives. You show them that life is about continuous growth, that curiosity has no age limit, and that wisdom is a blend of old and new. By being informed, learning new skills, embracing modern technology, and understanding today's parenting dynamics, you not only remain relevant but also become a trusted guide and role model for them. Your commitment to growth and education leaves a lasting legacy that will impact them for years to come.

We may not be rich and famous, but our Grandchildren are priceless.

Chapter Thirteen

Writing Letters for the Future.

The world is changing my dear grandchild, here is my hope for you and my gift to you.

My Dearest [Grandchild's Name],

In a world that seems to change with every breath, there is so much I want to share with you, so much wisdom I hope will comfort and guide you. The changes we witness—the ones that reach deep into the heart of our society—can be unsettling and, at times, overwhelming. But remember this, my precious grandchild: within you lies a strength that is boundless, a light that no darkness can extinguish. You are more powerful than you know because God's hand is always upon you.

I see that strength in your eyes, in the way they shine with hope and determination. I feel it in your embrace, that quiet, enduring energy that whispers, "I am here, and I am ready." You carry within you the resilience that has sustained our family for generations, and it is this same resilience that will see you through any storm.

Remember these words from Isaiah 41:10: "Fear not, for I am with you; be not dismayed, for I am your God. I will strengthen you, I will help you, I will uphold you with my righteous right hand." I share this with you, not to dismiss the fears and uncertainties you may feel, but to remind you of the divine power that surrounds you, guides you, and strengthens you through every challenge.

The world is like a tapestry constantly being woven and rewoven, each thread representing new opportunities, changes, and sometimes, challenges. There will be moments when the world feels heavy and the path ahead seems unclear. When those moments come, I want you to close your eyes, breathe deeply, and find the stillness within. Focus on what you can hold close—your faith, your kindness, the love you give and receive, and the wisdom you seek.

Embrace the journey of learning, for it is through seeking knowledge and understanding that we grow closer to God and closer to ourselves. Surround yourself with those who love you—your family, friends, and those who uplift you with their wisdom and encouragement. They will be your guiding lights, especially when the road ahead feels dark.

And my dear grandchild, never lose hope. The future may seem uncertain, but remember that God is with you always, and you have the power to shape the world with His love and grace. You and your generation are the authors of tomorrow, with the power to create a story filled with compassion, justice, and beauty.

As St. Augustine once said, "Faith is to believe what you do not see; the reward of this faith is to see what you believe." Take life one step at a time, knowing that each step is guided by divine love. With each step you take, know that I am with you, my love is with you, and God is with you. Keep moving forward, knowing you are never alone.

No matter how the world changes, our bond remains unbreakable. I am your grandma, and you are my heart. Together, we will navigate this ever-evolving world, guided by love, faith, and unwavering hope.

With all my love,
Grandma

This is just a sample letter, to get you started. I write letters to my grandchildren every few months and send them in the mail. They love getting these letters – after all nothing really comes in the mail for them – take the time to do this, because your grandchildren will love it.

I also have letters to each of my grandchildren for their future – writing letters to your grandchildren is a gift they will cherish one day.

Becoming a grandmother means my heart grows bigger with every little giggle.

Chapter Fourteen

Tweens, Teens and More.

Navigating the Journey of Tweens, Teens, and Grandparenting

As grandmothers, we are blessed with the gift of watching our grandchildren grow from innocent toddlers into vibrant teenagers. This stage of life—the tween and teen years—can be turbulent, but it's also filled with deep currents of change, self-discovery, and transformation. Maneuvering through these years as a grandmother requires love, patience, and adaptability. It is both beautiful and complex, a dance of connection and distance, where we must find our place in the lives of young people who are learning to navigate their own worlds.

The One-Word Response: How to Break Through the Wall

If you've ever tried to engage with a teenage grandchild only to receive a monosyllabic response like "fine" or "good," you're not alone. Tweens and teens are notorious for building walls, especially when it comes to conversations with adults. It can feel like they've shut you out, and that may stir a longing for the days when they would eagerly run into your arms, chattering away about their adventures.

But here's the thing: beneath those one-word responses are emotions and thoughts swirling inside them. Sometimes, it's less about what they're saying and more about being there, offering a steady presence. Your role as a grandmother is to remain patient and persistent. Don't be discouraged by the briefness of their words. Instead, create safe spaces where they feel comfortable to talk when they are ready. Ask open-ended questions when the moment is right and share your own stories. Sharing your experiences from your teenage years can help bridge the gap—letting them know you've been there, too.

Embracing Their Emotional Swings: How to Be a Steady Anchor

Emotions run wild during the teenage years. One moment they may be full of joy, the next weighed down by confusion or sadness. Hormones, peer pressures, and the overwhelming journey of self-discovery can cause these emotional swings. It can feel like you're on a rollercoaster as a grandmother, unsure of how to offer support without intruding.

Remember this: while you can't fix everything, your presence matters. Let your grandchild know they are loved and accepted for who they are. Avoid offering solutions immediately; instead, listen with compassion. Sometimes all they need is a soft place to land, a reminder that you are their steady anchor in the storm.

When emotions seem unmanageable, remind yourself that this too shall pass. A simple hug or a quiet walk together can do wonders for the soul. The warmth of your love, your patience, and your wisdom can serve as a guiding light during their most difficult days. You may not have all the answers, but your empathy will resonate with them, even when they don't show it.

Grandmother to a Teenage Girl: Fostering Connection in New Ways

Being a grandmother to a teenage girl comes with its own set of nuances. She may be on a quest to find her own identity, balancing the pressures of friendships, academics, and her evolving sense of self. It's easy to feel like you're losing touch with her as she grows into her independence, but this is a pivotal time to strengthen your relationship in ways that honor her individuality.

Engage her on topics she's passionate about. Be curious, ask her about her dreams, her thoughts on the world, and her friendships. Share your wisdom, but also show a willingness to learn from her. Teenage girls are often testing boundaries, and being non-judgmental, open, and supportive will keep the channels of communication flowing.

Encourage her to embrace her strengths and remind her that confidence and self-worth come from within. Your words will hold weight, even if they don't immediately appear to take root. Your love and belief in her will nurture the foundation for her to thrive as a young woman.

Grandmother to a Teenage Boy: Guiding with Strength and Compassion

With teenage boys, there may be times when the silence feels even more profound. They may withdraw, spending more time with friends or isolating themselves. It's crucial to give them space, but also to let them know you're there whenever they need you.

Sometimes, connecting with a teenage boy may happen during shared activities. Whether it's taking a walk, playing a game, or working on a project together, these moments of shared experience can open up opportunities for deeper conversations. Show him that it's okay to be vulnerable and remind him that strength comes in many forms—through kindness, empathy, and love.

The Lasting Impact of a Grandmother's Love

As a grandmother to tweens and teens, the path isn't always straightforward, but it is meaningful. Your patience, your quiet guidance, your unconditional love—these will remain with them, long after the one-word answers and emotional swings have faded. You are a constant in a world that can sometimes feel overwhelming for them. The seeds of love and wisdom you plant today will bloom in their hearts for years to come.

Chapter Fifteen

From 'Kicks' to 'Yeet'
A Grandmother's Guide to Teen Slang.

Understanding the ever-evolving language of today's teenagers can feel like learning a whole new language, but it's a fun and worthwhile journey!

Teen slang is more than just trendy words; it's a peek into their world, a way to express themselves, and a tool to connect with their peers. By getting to know some of these popular and playful slang terms, grandmothers can bridge the generational gap, spark more engaging conversations, and share a good laugh with their grandkids.

Whether you want to understand what they're saying or surprise them by using the lingo yourself, this list of 20 current slang words will help you stay in the loop and show that you're not just a loving grandma— you're a hip one, too!

- **Kicks** - Refers to sneakers or new shoes. "Check out my new kicks!"
- **Drip** - Describes a cool or stylish outfit or overall look. "He's got serious drip with that jacket."
- **Cap** - Means a lie or something that isn't true. "No cap" means "I'm not lying." "That's cap, there's no way that happened!"

- Sus - Short for "suspicious." Used to describe someone or something that seems off or shady. "That sounds a bit sus to me."
- Flex - To show off, usually in a boastful way. "He's always trying to flex his new phone."
- Slaps - Used to describe something that is amazing or really good, often music. "This song slaps!"
- Glow up - Refers to someone who has undergone a positive transformation, particularly in terms of appearance or style. "She had a major glow up over the summer."
- Fam - A way to refer to close friends or people who feel like family. "What's up, fam?"
- Bet - Means "okay" or "yes," often used to agree to something. "Wanna hang out later?" "Bet."
- Salty - Describes someone who is bitter or upset about something minor. "She's salty because she lost the game."
- Lit - Used to describe something that is exciting or fun. "That party was lit!"
- Bussin' - Refers to something really good, especially food. "This pizza is bussin'!"
- GOAT - Stands for "Greatest of All Time." "Serena Williams is the GOAT."
- Tea - Refers to gossip or the latest news. "Spill the tea, what happened at the party?"
- Vibe - Describes the mood or atmosphere of a place or person. "I'm loving the chill vibe here."
- Shook - Feeling surprised, shocked, or in disbelief. "I was shook when I heard the news!"
- Fire - Used to describe something that is really good or amazing. "That new track is fire!"

- **Savage** - Describes someone who is bold or doesn't care about consequences, often used in a funny way. "She roasted him in front of everyone; that was savage!"
- **Simp** - Someone who does too much for someone they like, often to the point of looking desperate. "He's such a simp for doing all her homework."
- **Yeet** - A versatile word used to express excitement or to throw something with force. "He yeeted the ball across the field!"

I have to say these slang words just make me laugh. ☺

Chapter Sixteen

Ignite Your Grandchild's Imagination With These 50 Questions.

Turn ordinary conversations into extraordinary adventures with 50 creative questions that will delight and surprise your grandchild! Discover their wildest dreams, silliest ideas, and hidden talents as you explore new worlds together. These prompts are the perfect way to inspire deeper connections and endless fun!

My grandsons always tell me they have the best conversations with me.

Here are 50 conversation starters to help you bond with your grandchild, in a fun and engaging way:

1. If you could have any superpower, what would it be and why?
2. What's the most exciting dream you've ever had?
3. If you could invent a new holiday, what would it be called and how would we celebrate it?
4. If animals could talk, which one do you think would be the funniest to talk to?
5. What's something you're really proud of that you've done recently?
6. If you could travel to any planet in the solar system, which one would you choose?

7. What's the weirdest food you've ever tried, and did you like it?
8. If you could switch places with any character from a book or movie, who would it be?
9. If you could create your own video game, what would it be about?
10. What's the most interesting fact you know?
11. If you could have a pet dinosaur, which one would you pick?
12. What's the first thing you would do if you were invisible for a day?
13. If you could be any age for a week, what age would you be and why?
14. If you could build the perfect playground, what would it look like?
15. What's your favorite joke? Can you tell me?
16. If you could learn any skill instantly, what would you want to learn?
17. What do you think the world will be like in 50 years?
18. If you could have any three wishes (and no wishing for more wishes!), what would they be?
19. If you were a superhero, what would your costume look like?
20. What's your favorite way to spend a rainy day?
21. If you could only eat one food for the rest of your life, what would it be?
22. If you could create a new animal, what would it look like and what would it be called?
23. If you could time travel, would you go to the past or the future? Why?
24. What's the coolest thing you've learned in school recently?

25. If you could make a new rule that everyone in the world had to follow, what would it be?
26. What's your favorite thing to do with friends?
27. If you could live inside any video game, which one would it be?
28. What would your perfect day look like from start to finish?
29. If you could invent a new ice cream flavor, what would it be?
30. If you had a robot, what would you want it to do for you?
31. What's something that makes you laugh every time?
32. If you could meet any famous person, who would it be and what would you ask them?
33. What's your favorite memory of us together?
34. If you could have any animal as a pet (even a wild one), what would you choose?
35. What's the most interesting place you've ever been?
36. If you were a teacher for a day, what would you teach?
37. What's a mystery you'd like to solve one day?
38. If you could make a movie, what would it be about?
39. What's something new you'd like to try this year?
40. If you could decorate your room any way you want, what would it look like?
41. What would you do if you found a treasure map?
42. If you could write a book, what would the story be about?
43. What's your favorite thing about your best friend?
44. If you could create your own board game, what would it be like?
45. What would you do if you could fly for a day?
46. What's one thing you're really good at that not many people know about?
47. If you could be a character in any TV show, who would you be?

48. What's something you've always wanted to learn but haven't yet?
49. If you could make one rule for our family, what would it be?
50. If you could design a new theme park, what would it be like?

These questions are designed to spark imagination, curiosity, and deeper connections with your grandchild!

Chapter Seventeen

The Special Bond between Grandmothers and their Granddaughters.

There's nothing quite like the relationship between grandmothers and their granddaughters. It's an unspoken connection that transcends generations, a bond woven with love, wisdom, and shared dreams. This sacred relationship is like a golden thread running through the fabric of life, stitching together past, present, and future. To witness it is to understand that some ties are eternal, and some love defies the limitations of time.

A Dance of Two Souls

In the presence of her grandmother, a granddaughter finds a kindred spirit—someone who not only offers unconditional love but also embodies the wisdom of lived experience. The grandmother sees her granddaughter not just as a young girl but as a reflection of her own youth. In her, she sees not just potential, but the evolution of the hopes and dreams she once carried. This bond is like a dance, fluid and graceful, filled with both laughter and learning, vulnerability and strength. It is the meeting of two souls at different stages of life, yet deeply in sync with one another.

From the earliest moments, when a granddaughter grasps her grandmother's hand, something shifts in the heart of both. For the grandmother, it's a connection to the future, a continuation of her legacy. For the granddaughter, it's the assurance of safety and warmth, of stories shared and memories yet to be made. It's as though they are entwined in an invisible embrace, a hug that stretches across the years.

A Keeper of Stories

Grandmothers are the keepers of stories, of family lore and personal histories. In a world that often rushes forward, they are the ones who hold the past with gentle reverence, offering it like a gift to their granddaughters. They pass on not just traditions, but the wisdom of their lived experiences. Through tales told over tea, or during a quiet walk, grandmothers impart lessons that can't be learned from books or screens.

It's in these moments that the granddaughter learns not only about her heritage but also about resilience and grace. From the stories of a grandmother's struggles and triumphs, she learns how to navigate her own challenges. She learns that life, with all its ups and downs, is a journey best traveled with an open heart and a steady spirit. There is a quiet power in these exchanges, one that shapes the granddaughter's sense of self and place in the world.

The Quiet Understanding

The bond between grandmothers and granddaughters is marked by a quiet understanding. It is an unspoken recognition of shared womanhood, of strength passed down through generations. In each other's presence, they can be themselves, free from judgment or expectation. The grandmother, having lived through the stages her granddaughter is now experiencing, offers a unique perspective. She listens with a patience born of time and offers guidance that is neither overbearing nor condescending.

For the granddaughter, this connection is a source of comfort. It is a refuge from the often chaotic world of growing up, a place where she can simply be. The grandmother's presence is a reminder that she is part of something larger, that the challenges she faces have been faced before, and will be faced again by those who come after her. This cyclical nature of their relationship is a grounding force, a reminder that no matter where life takes them, they are never truly alone.

The Gift of Time

One of the greatest gifts a grandmother can give her granddaughter is her time. In a world that seems to move faster by the day, a grandmother offers the gift of slowing down. Whether it's teaching her how to bake a beloved family recipe, working on a puzzle together, or simply sitting side by side in comfortable silence, these moments are precious. They are the building blocks of memories that will last a lifetime, shaping not only the granddaughter's childhood but also the woman she will become.

It's in these shared moments that the granddaughter learns the importance of patience, of paying attention to the small details of life. She learns that not everything needs to be rushed, that there is beauty in taking time to savor the little things. From her grandmother, she learns the art of presence—of being fully engaged in the moment, whether it's laughing together or quietly reflecting.

A Bond That Grows

As a granddaughter grows into adulthood, the bond with her grandmother does not fade; it evolves. What was once a relationship of nurturing and guidance transforms into one of mutual respect and admiration. The granddaughter, now with her own experiences and wisdom, can offer her grandmother the same support and love she once received. In this phase, they become not just family, but friends— two women, bound by love and shared history, walking side by side.

In the later years of life, this bond can become even more profound. A granddaughter may find herself caring for her grandmother, offering the same tenderness and support she was given in her youth. It's a beautiful, full-circle moment, one that speaks to the enduring nature of their relationship.

A Love Beyond Words

The bond between grandmothers and granddaughters is a love that defies words. It is a connection that is felt more than spoken, a deep-rooted understanding that transcends age and time. It is a bond that celebrates the power of womanhood, the strength of family, and the beauty of shared experience.

As we celebrate this sacred relationship, we are reminded that grandmothers and granddaughters are more than just relatives. They are soul companions, forever linked by love, wisdom, and the shared journey of life. Their bond is a testament to the power of family and the enduring nature of love across generations. Truly, there is nothing quite like it.

Chapter Eighteen

Grandmothers and their Grandsons, have a special relationship.

A granddaughter brings a sweetness all her own, like a delicate flower blooming with grace, curiosity, and tenderness, **while a grandson arrives like a burst of energy, full of playful spirit and bold adventur**e. Both are woven from the same thread of love, yet their presence unfolds in beautifully distinct ways. The granddaughter's soft giggles and quiet confidences create moments of gentle wonder, while the grandson's mischievous laughter and boundless curiosity light up a grandmother's heart with excitement. Each brings their own magic—her quiet strength and his fearless joy—and together they shape a grandmother's world in ways as unique as the stars in the sky.

From the moment a grandmother first lays eyes on her grandson, there is an immediate sense of wonder and awe. Her heart swells with a love so profound, it's difficult to put into words. Unlike her experience as a mother, where responsibilities and worries sometimes overwhelmed the sheer joy of parenting, being a grandmother allows her to savor each moment with her grandson in a new, more relaxed way. Grandmothers often say that becoming a grandparent is like receiving a second chance to experience the magic of childhood—this time, without the pressures of daily parenting.

For the grandson, the relationship with his grandmother is equally magical. A grandmother's love is often pure, untainted by the rules and discipline that come with parenting. She is a figure of comfort and safety, a soft place to land after the bumps of childhood. Whether she's telling stories, baking cookies, or simply offering a listening ear, a grandmother provides a unique kind of emotional sanctuary. She brings patience and understanding, qualities often honed through years of life experience, that create a sense of security for her grandson.

One of the key elements that make this relationship so special is the transfer of wisdom across generations. A grandmother has lived through decades of change and growth, yet in her heart, she often remains connected to the childlike wonder that comes from experiencing life with fresh eyes. Through her, grandsons learn valuable lessons—not just about family history or life skills, but also about resilience, kindness, and the importance of relationships. Grandmothers share stories from their past, reminding their grandsons of the rich legacy they are part of, while also teaching them to cherish the simple, timeless joys of life.

Grandmothers also provide a sense of stability and continuity in an ever-changing world. In today's fast-paced society, where technology, trends, and expectations shift rapidly, a grandmother often embodies the values of patience, hard work, and perseverance. For her grandsons, she becomes a touchstone, a reminder of the enduring power of love and family. She may impart old-world traditions—whether it's in the form of a cherished recipe, a family heirloom, or a special way of celebrating holidays—that create lasting memories and a sense of connection to their roots.

But it's not just about the lessons and traditions. There's a pure, unbridled joy that grandmothers and grandsons share. Whether they're playing in the yard, laughing over a silly joke, or discovering something new together, the fun and laughter they experience form some of the sweetest memories. This relationship brings out a side of grandmothers that is playful and carefree, reminding them of the importance of staying young at heart. For grandsons, having someone who both encourages their imagination and indulges their sense of fun is a priceless gift.

This bond also has a spiritual dimension. It is often said that grandparents are bridges to the past while helping their grandchildren navigate the present. For grandsons, their grandmother's presence symbolizes unconditional love and acceptance, which gives them the confidence to explore the world and embrace who they are.

In the end, the magic of the relationship between a grandmother and her grandsons is about more than just love—it's about connection, legacy, and shared joy. It's the whispered words of encouragement, the shared adventures, and the knowledge that no matter where life takes them, they'll always carry a piece of each other in their hearts. This relationship is a true gift, one that enriches both their lives in ways that are irreplaceable and everlasting.

Twenty-One Things They Didn't Tell Me about Being a Grandmother

1. **The magnetic pull of "Grandma's House"**: How obsessed your grandchildren will become with their grandmothers, and how visiting your house will always feel like the greatest adventure.

2. **A love beyond comprehension**: What it truly means to experience love on another level—a love that feels more unconditional than you ever imagined.

3. **Tension with in-laws**: The subtle (or not-so-subtle) jealousy that may arise from your son- or daughter-in-law over your bond with the grandchildren. It may simmer or flash in their expressions, but it's often there.

4. **Unexpected jealousy from your own child**: Seeing your grown child feel left out or envious of the closeness you share with their children can be heartbreaking yet surprising.

5. **Biting your tongue is a skill**: Keeping quiet is harder than you'd think, especially when you don't agree. After all, they're not *your* kids anymore, but your child's.

6. **Your advice is an optional extra**: While they may politely listen, your advice is often taken as mere input—ultimately, they have their own way of doing things, which they believe is better.

7. **You're not alone**: Many grandmothers around the world feel the same challenges and joys—this emotional roller coaster is a shared experience.

8. **Letting go of personal sensitivities**: You quickly learn that you can't take things too personally—parenting styles, decisions, or even your grandchild's moods.

9. **They belong to their parents**: The deep connection with your grandchildren can sometimes make you forget that they are not your own children; they belong to your child and their partner.

10. **Different parenting philosophies**: You may witness parenting choices that you completely disagree with. Whether it's discipline or lifestyle, you'll have to step back and let them be in charge.

11. **Their health, their way**: How to care for sick grandchildren is firmly in the parents' domain. While suggestions may be welcomed, decisions will ultimately follow their preferences.

12. **Your house, your rules, but...** You may want to spoil them with treats and TV, but respecting the parents' rules (even in your home) can sometimes lead to friction.

13. **How protective you'll feel**: You may think parenting made you fiercely protective, but grandmotherhood brings that instinct to an even more intense level.

14. **Relearning patience**: Having little ones around again will test your patience in ways that are very different from when you raised your own kids.

15. **The constant need for boundaries**: It's harder than expected to set boundaries, not just with the grandkids, but with their parents too.

16. **Feeling sidelined during family conflicts**: Sometimes, despite your best intentions, you'll feel like an outsider in family disagreements.

17. **How much you'll miss them**: When they're not around, the house feels empty in a new way. The longing to see them can be more intense than you ever thought possible.

18. **Modern technology's role**: You'll learn new ways to connect with them through FaceTime, social media, and text messaging. It's a different world than when you raised your children!

19. **Worrying about them as teens**: It doesn't stop after their childhood—grandmothers worry about their grandchildren's teenage struggles just as much as their parents do.

20. **Balancing fairness between grandchildren**: You'll feel the need to treat all your grandchildren equally, but some bonds will inevitably be stronger, and that can create tension.

21. **The emotional rollercoaster of letting go**: As they grow older, especially into their teen years, letting them go and become their own person can feel like losing a piece of your heart all over again.

Your Legacy Begins...

As you close the final pages of this book and step fully into your role as a grandmother, know that you are now part of a remarkable generation of women who shape and inspire the lives of the next generation. You stand alongside countless grandmothers who, like you, have embraced this journey with open arms, knowing the role is both a privilege and a calling.

Together, we are part of a lineage that embodies strength, compassion, and quiet wisdom—a generation of grandmothers who understand that to love fiercely is to leave a legacy that will live on long after we are gone.

As grandmothers, we are the keepers of family stories, the healers of hurts, and the custodians of traditions that will ground and guide the little ones who look to us with eyes full of wonder. In a world that often feels fast and ever-changing, we are a constant, a reminder of what truly matters. We are the steady voice of wisdom, the gentle hand that guides, and the warm embrace that assures them they are loved.

I hope the insights, and advice shared in these pages have been helpful to you —they are gifts from those who have walked this path before you, each one a thread in the intricate tapestry of grandmotherhood.

Let me remind you that, while the road ahead may be winding, it is filled with meaning and joy. Remember that being a grandmother is about more than just sharing time; it's about sharing your life, your values, and the love that makes each day meaningful.

So, go forward boldly. Be great not only in your deeds but in your spirit. Be a woman who listens with understanding, who loves without limits, and who stands as a pillar of grace and strength. Let your grandchildren see in you the beauty of resilience, the joy of curiosity, and the warmth of acceptance. Let them feel, in your every hug and whispered word, the love that runs so deep it needs no explanation.

Cherish every moment, grandmother to be. Know that you are a gift, a precious instant that will one day become part of the memories your grandchildren hold close to their hearts. The laughter you share today, the stories you tell, and the love you give—all of these will stay with them as they grow. They will remember the smell of cookies in your kitchen, the sound of your laughter, the comfort of your arms around them when the world feels too big.

As you walk this journey, know that you are creating something timeless and beautiful. You are part of a generation that doesn't just witness history—you create it in the lives you touch and the hearts you shape. So go forth with joy, knowing you are part of something larger than yourself, something that will echo through time. **You are living your legacy, one small hand held, one story shared, and one moment of love at a time.**

Now, go, dear grandmother to be—embrace this journey fully and leave your beautiful, unforgettable mark on the life of each of your grandchildren!

Congratulations on becoming a Grandmother!!!!

Don't forget to join us when you become a grandmother at:

www.moderngrandmothers.com

Modern
Grandmothers

Printed in Great Britain
by Amazon